Corporate Finance:

A Simple Introduction

Also by K.H. Erickson

Simple Introductions

Accounting and Finance Formulas
Applied Econometrics
Choice Theory
Corporate Finance
Corporate Finance Formulas
eBay
Econometrics
Economics
Environmental Economics
Financial Economics
Financial Risk Management
Game Theory
Game Theory for Business
International Relations
Investment Appraisal
Investment Formulas
Marketing Management Concepts and Tools
Mathematical Formulas for Economics and Business
Methods of Microeconomics
Microeconomics
Security Valuation

Corporate Finance:

A Simple Introduction

K.H. Erickson

© 2018 K.H. Erickson

All rights reserved.

No part of this publication may be reproduced, stored in or introduced into a retrieval system, or transmitted in any form or by any means, including electronic, mechanical, photocopying, recording or otherwise, without the prior permission of the author.

Contents

1 Introduction — 6

2 Capital Structure — 8

2.1 Firm Value and the Cost of Capital — 8

2.2 Traditional Theory of Capital Structure — 12

2.3 The Theory of No Optimal Capital Structure — 16

2.4 The Effects of Taxation — 24

2.5 Market Imperfections — 31

3 Dividend Policy — 37

3.1 Dividend Irrelevance Theory — 37

3.2 The Dividend Decision — 42

3.3 Share Repurchases — 47

4 Option Theory — 50

4.1 Options Contracts — 50

4.2 Black-Scholes Option Pricing Model — 61

4.3 Options Strategies — 65

5 Mergers and Acquisitions — 71

5.1 Merger Basics — 71

5.2 Merger Motivations — 74

5.3 Merger Methods and Takeover Tactics — 80

5.4 The Value Impact of Mergers — 89

6 Bibliography — 97

1 Introduction

Corporate Finance is the field of a company that deals with its financial and investment decisions. A company must evaluate the relative benefits of equity and debt funding, and decide on its capital structure, and a chapter on this subject details the difference between debt and equity and how this can affect a firm's value. First, the traditional theory is put forward, that there is an optimal capital structure and level of debt, before Modigliani and Miller's theory that there is no optimal capital structure, as any benefits brought about by taking on debt are cancelled out by rising equity costs. The remainder of the chapter looks at the effect that the realities of corporate and personal taxes, asymmetric information, financial distress, and agency costs have on the theory of capital structure.

Shareholders are the owners of a company, and a chapter on dividend policy looks into how managers may attempt to increase shareholder value. The theory that the dividend payout ratio is irrelevant as shareholders can create their own dividends is put forward, before the idea that investors' interpretation of firm policy may influence the dividend decision. Share repurchases are a popular method of returning profits to shareholders, and a section explains the benefits associated with this policy.

Companies are exposed to price volatility and risk in their daily activities, and often use financial derivatives to reduce and hedge against this risk, or to profit from it, and a chapter on options details how this is performed. European and American calls and puts are explained, with diagrams and numerical examples detailing what an investor requires to generate a profit. A section on the Black-Scholes Option Pricing Model shows how European call and put options are priced, and the factors determining increases or decreases in this price. Various option strategies are then detailed with diagrams and numerical examples, to show how speculators, hedgers, or arbitrageurs can use options to profit from price volatility, eliminate risk, or generate risk-free profits respectively.

Mergers and acquisitions are an important field of corporate finance, and common motivations for mergers are explained, along with some situations where they may be beneficial and some where they may not. The process a firm goes through to undertake a merger or acquisition is detailed, with the relative benefits of cash and share funding assessed, relative value ratio and exchange ratio calculations explained, and possible takeover defence strategies presented. Finally, the value impact of mergers on different groups is examined, with empirical evidence on why mergers and acquisitions may disappoint looked at using alternative theories.

2 Capital Structure

2.1 Firm Value and the Cost of Capital

The market value of a firm equals the market value of its equity added to the market value of its debt. Equity refers to a stock or other security which represents an ownership interest, and the equity value on a company's balance sheet will equal the total of owners or shareholders' funds, and retained earnings or losses. Debt refers to borrowed funds, and the debt value on a balance sheet will be the total sum of money due to be paid to others, either in the short-term (current liabilities) or loans to be paid back in the long-term (non-current liabilities).

A firm can increase its equity value by selling more shares to investors, which gives others a share of ownership over the company in return for their money. And a firm can increase its debt value by increasing its liabilities, either privately via taking bank loans or publicly by selling investors bonds which guarantee regular interest payments and/or a payoff at maturity. As these options will both offer a future stream of earnings for a firm, either from shareholders or from a bank or bond investors, each may to be used increase a firm's market value.

The sum ($\sum$) of a firm's stream of earnings for each time period t (X_t), discounted by Q the appropriate discount rate [1 / (1+ Q)] which is weighted for the time period (^{t}), gives a firm's value:

$$\text{Firm Value, } V = \sum [X_t / (1 + Q)^t]$$

Discounting of earnings is required due to the time value of money, where a sum of money to be received in the future is worth less than if the same sum of money was received today. This is because future earnings are expected to always be higher than current earnings due to interest or other profitable investment opportunities. The appropriate discount rate, Q, to use to make earnings received at different time periods in the future comparable is a firm's cost of capital, k (Q = k). This refers to the opportunity cost for a firm when it uses its capital (i.e. financial resources) for a specific investment, and it is the next best return (for the same level of risk) forgone when an investment is made.

For example, if a firm plans to use $50,000 for an investment project with zero risk, and the current rate of interest offered by a bank (i.e. the risk-free rate of interest) is 3%, then the firm's cost of capital is 3%. The firm must forgo a guaranteed 3% return in bank interest that could have been made on the $50,000 if the money is used for an alternative investment project instead, and therefore the investment's earnings must be discounted by 3% to make a realistic assessment of its actual performance. If a firm invests in stock with a 5% level of risk (i.e. the standard deviation or volatility of returns from the stock's average return is 5%), the firm's cost of capital is the percentage return associated with the best performing alternative stock which has the same 5% level of risk.

The cost of capital (k) is also known as the required rate of return, as it refers to the rate of return required by a firm or investor to cover the opportunity cost of spending money which could have been used on alternative investments. If a firm is financed entirely by equity the cost of capital will equal the cost of equity, and the return required by shareholders in the firm. And if the firm is financed entirely by debt the cost of capital will equal the cost of debt, and the interest rate that the firm must pay on its debt obligations (e.g. bank loans and bond payments). When a firm is funded by more than one source the cost of capital is the weighted average of the costs associated with the sources of the funds, weighted by the proportion each source represents of the total funds. The weighted average cost of capital (WACC) or cost of capital for short (k) can be found with the formula:

$$k = k_E (V_E / V) + k_D (V_D / V)$$

Where k_E is the cost of equity, k_D is the cost of debt, V_E is the firm's equity value, V_D is the firm's debt value, and V is the total firm value with $V = V_E + V_D$.

A firm's investment must generate a return equal to the cost of capital in the medium term, to cover the (opportunity) cost of financing the investment. It would therefore be advantageous for a firm for the cost of capital to be lower, to reduce the level of investment return required to cover their costs, making this more likely to be achieved. A lower cost of capital would of course also increase firm value, by reducing the discount rate for future streams of earnings. The next section looks into the idea that a firm can indeed reduce its cost of capital, by altering its capital structure and changing the proportions of equity and debt used to fund its operations.

2.2 Traditional Theory of Capital Structure

The last section explained that the cost of debt is the interest rate a company must pay on its borrowed money, while the cost of equity is the return required by shareholders. As a firm is legally obliged to pay its debt holders before its shareholders, and as debt holders are promised they will get the initial money they loaned (i.e. the principal) back while shareholders holding equity receive no such promise, debt holders take on less risk than equity holders. Whatever chance there is of a debt holder not getting paid, the chance is greater for an equity holder. To make up for taking on this greater risk equity holders will demand a greater return than debt holders, and this ensures that the required rate of return for shareholders, the cost of equity, is always greater than the cost of debt.

As debt always costs less than equity followers of the traditional view of capital structure see the potential for the overall cost of capital to be reduced, and firm value increased, if a firm takes on more debt and increases the proportion of its capital structure funded by debt relative to equity. Traditionalists acknowledge that a firm taking on more debt will increase the risks that a shareholder in the firm is exposed to, pushing shareholders to increase their required rate of return and raise the cost of equity. But the traditional view is that at low levels of debt this risk increase for shareholders is negligible, and therefore their required rate of return and the cost of equity will only rise slightly. There is therefore a net gain from taking on debt, as slight increases in the cost of equity are outweighed by significantly lower costs of debt.

The traditional view of capital structure is that taking on debt is only beneficial with low levels of debt however, and as the proportion of a firm funded by debt increases shareholders will raise their required rate of return and the cost of equity by greater and greater amounts, as they seek compensation for the ever higher risk they face. As noted at the start of this section debt holders must be paid before equity shareholders, and therefore the more debt a firm takes on the higher risk there is that a firm's money will run out before equity holders are paid. Another cause of the cost of equity jumping significantly with higher levels of debt is that the cost of debt, which the cost of equity will always exceed, rises with high levels of debt. As a firm takes on too many debt obligations it will struggle to pay them all, forcing creditors to raise the return they demand for further loans (i.e. the cost of debt) as the risk of the loans not being repaid has increased. Therefore at some level of debt the benefits associated with the cost of debt being lower than the cost of equity will be outweighed by rises in the equity holders' required rate of return, and the optimal capital structure has the level of debt kept below this. The following diagram explains this idea of an optimal capital structure in visual form.

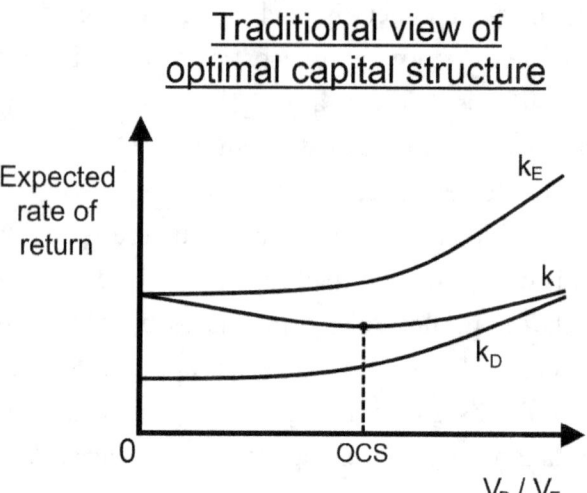

With zero debt and a firm financed entirely by equity at the far left of the graph the cost of capital, k, is equal to the cost of equity, k_E. But as lower cost debt is taken on with a movement rightwards in the diagram the cost of capital, k, declines, highlighting the benefits of taking on debt. This decline in the cost of capital (and resulting rise in firm value) continues until the point marked OCS, which stands for optimal capital structure. This is where the required rate of return and cost of capital is at its lowest as the k curve clearly shows. Rightwards of this point, with higher debt levels, the cost of equity rises by ever greater amounts and the cost of debt, k_D, rises too, both pushing up the overall cost of capital and reducing firm value. This continues until the firm is almost completely funded by debt and the costs of debt and capital converge at the far right of the graph.

Traditional capital structure theory is based on a number of assumptions. Only equity or debt financing is available to a firm, internal financing is not available. All earnings are assumed to be paid out as dividends to shareholders, no earnings are retained or reinvested. A firm's total assets and revenues are fixed, as is its financing. Investors are rational. And there are no taxes. The fixed financing assumption means that equity holders can't just sell their shares when a firm begins to take on more debt, while the rational investors assumption ensures they will demand a higher return for their shares as a firm takes on more debt and more risk. All earnings paid out as dividends, the unavailability of internal financing, and the fixed assets and revenues assumptions ensures that higher levels of debt are always associated with more risk, and a firm can't rely on increases in retained earnings, internal financing, or assets and revenue to pay increased debt obligations.

Evidence from the real world and common sense suggests that not all of the assumptions of traditional capital structure theory are likely to hold, and therefore some additional analysis is required to uncover the full picture on capital structure. The next section introduces a different theory, arguing that there may be no one optimal capital structure for a firm at all in certain circumstances.

2.3 The Theory of No Optimal Capital Structure

Modigliani and Miller (1958) put forward a theory that if financial markets operate perfectly then a firm's cost of capital will remain the same irrespective of its level of debt, and therefore there is no optimal capital structure which will offer a higher firm value. Modigliani and Miller acknowledge that the cost of debt will be lower than the cost of equity, as debt holders are given legal priority to be paid before equity holders, but they insisted that this doesn't mean that replacing equity capital with debt capital will lower the overall cost of capital.

M & M's theory of capital structure irrelevance has several assumptions, based on the idea of perfect capital markets. There are only two assets available to a firm; debt and equity. Firms can't go bankrupt, and the proportion of debt in a firm's capital structure doesn't raise the cost of debt or affect the cost of capital. Financial markets are frictionless, with zero flotation or transaction costs. Both insiders and outsiders, firm managers and investors, have access to the same set of information. Firm management acts exclusively to benefit shareholders. Investors are rational. Future cash flows and dividends are known. And there is no corporate or personal taxation. The assumptions noted are unlikely to all hold of course, but they show the factors which would determine an optimal capital structure.

The theory of capital structure irrelevance states that as equity is substituted for debt, the rate of return required by equity holders will rise by exactly the same amount as the gain from debt being cheaper than equity (and not less than this gain, as in traditional theory). This ensures the net effect of substituting equity for debt is zero. M & M stated that this occurs because in perfect capital markets individuals can duplicate the capital structure of firms themselves, using 'home-made leverage'. And if there is ever a time where the gain from replacing equity with debt exceeds the rise in the rate of return on equity then individual investors will quickly fix this through arbitrage.

For example, individuals at firm A where the rate of return on equity hasn't risen enough can simply sell shares they hold in the firm. Then take that money, and borrow to replicate their prior debt exposure (e.g. if they had held $1,000 in equity and firm A was 50% debt financed, they would borrow 1,000 x 0.5 = 500), then invest all of the $1,500 in a firm with no debt, firm B. This would generate a higher return for them than before even after debt interest payments, as firm A was not offering a rate of return on equity as high as they should be, for exactly the same level of debt risk as they had before with firm A, as corporate debt exposure is replaced with individual debt exposure. And this selling of shares would lower firm A's value via lower equity, and raise firm's B value via higher equity, negating what firm A was trying to do by taking on debt, until both firms had exactly the same firm value and the profit incentive for individuals to act this way was gone.

To further examine Modigliani and Miller's point on the irrelevance of capital structure in perfect capital markets imagine there are two firms, firm U which is unlevered with zero debt and only equity financed, and firm L which is levered with both debt and equity financing. Apart from this difference the two firms are identical. An individual investor can either (1) buy 10% of the shares of levered firm L; or (2) buy 10% of the shares of unlevered firm U and borrow funds equivalent to 10% of the debt of firm L. Investment option (1) generates investor income of the following, where F is the levered firm's earnings for the period, and D_L is the interest payments on the debt of firm L for the period:

$$0.1 \, (F - D_L)$$

Investment option (2) comprises of two actions. Borrowing funds equivalent to 10% of firm L's debt incurs a cost of:

$$- 0.1 \, D_L$$

And buying 10% of unlevered firm U generates investor income equal to 10% of the unlevered firm's earnings for the period. As the levered and unlevered firms are identical in all ways except for their level of debt this income equals:

$$0.1\ F$$

Putting both of investment (2)'s actions together gives:

$$0.1\ (F - D_L)$$

This is exactly the same investor income as investment (1), and therefore both investments offer the same income. Next the funding requirements of each investment option will be compared. The capital required to fund investment (1) is the cost of 10% of the levered firm L's shares, which is 10% of firm L's market value of equity:

$$0.1\ E_L$$

And the capital required to fund investment (2) is the cost of 10% of the unlevered firm U's shares, which is 10% of firm U's market value of equity:

$$0.1\ E_U$$

However, investment (2) also involved borrowing funds equivalent to 10% of firm L's debt, $0.1\ D_L$, and as this amount of capital will be borrowed it can be deducted from the total capital required to fund investment option

(2). This means the actual capital required to fund investment (2) is:

$$0.1 (E_U - D_L)$$

It has already been shown that the income an investor will receive from each of these two investment options is the same, with earnings of $0.1 (F - D_L)$. And risk is also the same with a debt exposure of $0.1 D_L$. In perfect capital markets the two investment options will therefore have the same value and the capital requirement will be the same:

$$0.1 E_L = 0.1 (E_U - D_L)$$

Multiplying both sides of this equation by 10 gives:

$$E_L = E_U - D_L$$

And rearranging gives:

$$E_L + D_L = E_U$$

This equation states that equity value of the levered firm, added to the debt value of the levered firm, equals the equity value of the unlevered firm. In other words, in perfect capital markets the value of a levered firm, V_L, is exactly equal the value of an unlevered firm, V_U:

$$V_L = V_U$$

This equation is the first proposition of Modigliani and Miller's theorem, that a firm's market value is independent of its capital structure in perfect capital markets. Increasing the proportion of debt in a capital structure doesn't affect a firm's value or its overall cost of capital, but only redistributes value from equity shareholders to creditors who own the debt.

The second proposition of Modigliani and Miller's theorem follows on logically from the implications of the first, stating that the rate of return on equity required by shareholders of a levered firm will increase in direct proportion to the debt-equity ratio:

$$k_E = k_{EU} + [(k_{EU} - k_D) \times (V_D / V_E)]$$

In this equation k_E is the cost of equity for a levered firm financed by both debt and equity, k_{EU} is the cost of equity for an unlevered firm financed solely by equity, k_D is the cost of debt, and V_D / V_E is the debt-equity ratio found by dividing the levered firm's value of debt by its value of equity. As the k_{EU} factor in this equation is determined only by the operating risk of the unlevered firm, and is unaffected by debt, it will be the relative level of debt and the debt-equity ratio, V_D / V_E, which drives changes in the rate of return on equity required by shareholders, k_E. This requires a constant cost of debt, k_D, of course, which depends on M & M's simplifying assumption that firms can't go bankrupt. Without that assumption the cost of debt, k_D, in the above equation would rise with higher levels of debt, as a firm takes on too many debt obligations and moves closer to potential bankruptcy. And the cost of debt rising would prevent M & M's second theorem from holding, as the rate of return on equity in the equation will no longer rise in direct proportion to the debt-equity ratio.

The following diagram represents the second proposition of M & M's theorem in visual form.

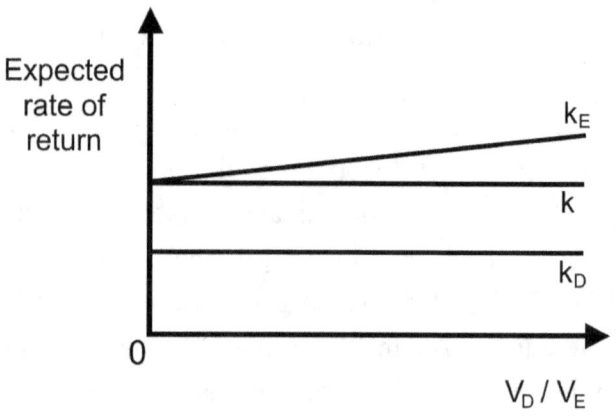

This shows that as the proportion of a firm's capital structure financed by debt (the debt-equity ratio, V_D / V_E)

increases the cost of equity (k_E) increases in direct proportion, as shown by the upward sloping but straight cost of equity line. This keeps the cost of capital (k) constant irrespective of the level of debt, showing that it is a firm's assets which determine the cost of capital not its method of financing. A constant cost of debt (k_D) is assumed.

The last two sections have shown that there may or may not be an optimal capital structure for a firm, largely depending on whether or not capital markets operate perfectly, and whether or not the cost of debt rises as the proportion of a firm's capital structure financed by debt reaches higher levels. But both theories presented so far, the traditional theory of capital structure and the theory of no optimal capital structure, have assumed there are no taxes. The next section relaxes this assumption and examines the effect taxation, both corporate and personal, can have on a firm's optimal capital structure.

2.4 The Effects of Taxation

Interest payments on debt can be deducted from corporate taxes, while earnings and dividend payments to shareholders with equity can't, and this offers a significant advantage to firms with debt. Two companies may have identical pre-tax cash flows, but if they have different capital structures they will pay different rates of corporate tax as debt offers a tax shield. For this reason levered companies (with debt) can be valued higher than unlevered companies (without debt), and therefore having a capital structure with more debt can be beneficial for a company.

The precise value of a levered company will equal the value of an unlevered company, plus the present value of the tax savings on debt which result from debt acting as a tax shield from corporate taxes. And this present value of the tax savings will increase with the amount of the debt and its maturity (as a longer maturity means more years of debt payments to act as a tax shield). Tax savings need to be adjusted from their original value into a present value due to the time value of money discussed earlier, but there are several potential options for the discount rate. The cost of equity could be used to discount tax savings, as the benefits the savings offer to a firm will go to equity shareholders, and the cost of equity will also change with circumstances to add flexibility to discounting. Alternatively, the cost of capital could be used to discount, as it reflects both the cost of equity and the cost of debt.

However, if debt is perpetual and the tax savings from debt acting as a tax shield are permanent then the cost of debt, k_D, is used as the discount rate. This means the value of the tax savings equals the corporate tax rate (T_C) multiplied by the cost of debt (k_D) multiplied by the value of debt (V_D), all divided by the cost of debt (k_D):

$$\text{Value of tax savings} = (T_C \times k_D \times V_D) / k_D$$

With the cost of debt term, k_D, on both the top and bottom of the equation the tax shield simplifies down to:

$$\text{Value of tax savings} = T_C \times V_D$$

If corporate taxes are present then the value of a levered firm (V_L) will always exceed the value of an unlevered firm (V_U). And the first proposition of Modigliani and Miller's theorem must be amended to account for the value of tax savings on debt. M & M's first proposition with corporate taxes therefore becomes:

$$\mathbf{V_L = V_U + (T_C \times V_D)}$$

The second proposition of M & M must also be amended if corporate taxes are present, and the cost of equity (k_E) formula is changed to account for the debt-equity ratio (V_D / V_E) after corporate tax (T_C) by multiplying it by ($1 - T_C$):

$$k_E = k_{EU} + [(k_{EU} - k_D) \times (V_D / V_E) \times (1 - T_C)]$$

The second proposition of Modigliani and Miller with corporate taxes is shown in visual form below. As in the model without corporate taxes perfect capital markets are assumed, and firms can't go bankrupt.

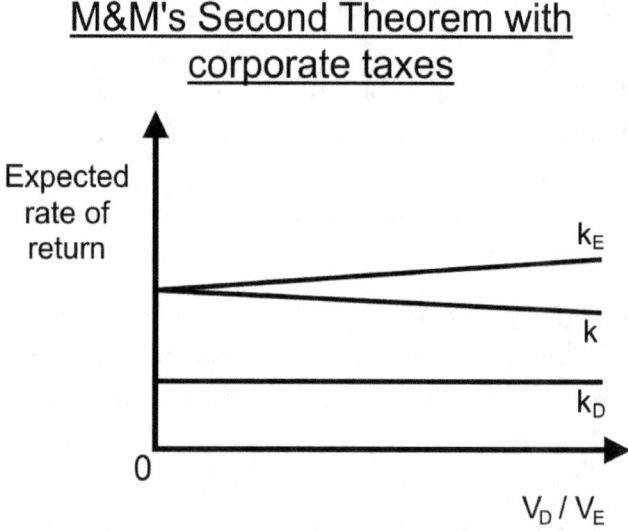

As a firm swaps equity for debt in its capital structure and the debt-equity ratio (V_D / V_E) increases, with a move right in the graph, the cost of equity (k_E) rises at a lower rate than it did in the model without taxes, although it still increases in direct proportion to the debt-equity ratio. However, when corporate taxes are present the cost of capital (k) falls with a higher debt-equity ratio, and instead of there being no optimal capital structure it is optimal for a firm to take on more debt to lower the cost of capital. This will lower the discount rate for firm value, and increase the market value of a firm.

This section has so far only examined corporate taxes, but they are not the only type of taxes which are linked to debt. While those who owe debt can use it to cut their corporate tax bill, the creditors who issue debt may have to pay personal taxes on their interest income. This will reduce the amount of money creditors actually receive in interest payments from firms, raising the total amount of money firms must pay on their debt in order to achieve their targeted net cost of debt. And the increased funds required to pay debt must come from a firm's resources, which reduces earnings for its shareholders. In many countries the tax on interest income is greater than the corporate tax rate, and Miller (1977) claimed that the taxes paid by investors on interest income can cancel out those paid by corporations, meaning that there is no benefit for a firm increasing its debt, and therefore no optimal capital structure.

The total effect of tax on optimal capital structure can be related to three different tax rates, the corporate tax rate, the personal tax on interest income, and the personal tax on stock income. The corporate tax rate rewards use of debt as debt is tax-deductible, while a higher personal tax on stock income (e.g. on dividends) also rewards use of debt over equity to avoid this tax. On the other hand a higher personal tax on interest income rewards use of equity over debt, to minimize that cost. The overall tax shield of debt is therefore given by the following formula, where T_C is the corporate tax rate, T_E is the tax on equity income, T_D is the tax on interest income for debt, and V_D is the market value of debt:

$$\text{Tax shield} = \{1 - [(1 - T_C) \times (1 - T_E)] / (1 - T_D)\} \times V_D$$

If $T_E = T_D$ then the tax shield of debt and the value of tax savings is the same as in the basic case, when only corporate tax rates are considered, and there is an incentive for a firm to take on debt to achieve an optimal capital structure.

If $T_E > T_D$ then the tax shield is greater than in the basic case, and there is a strong incentive for a firm to take on debt.

But if $T_E < T_D$ then the tax shield is smaller than in the basic case, and there may not be an incentive for a firm to take on debt, and there may not be an optimal capital structure.

With some combinations of the three different tax rates the total tax shield of debt may be very close to zero.

Graham (2000) found that when corporate taxes alone are included the tax shield offered by debt is 9.7 percent, but when personal taxes paid by an investor are also included the value of tax savings created by debt falls to 4.3 percent. Furthermore, Graham et al. (2004) finds that firms make large aggregate tax savings with employee stock option deductibles, which also affects corporate marginal tax rates, to suggest there are often better ways for a firm to lower its tax bill than taking on debt.

When personal taxes are included in the analysis the tax objective of firms changes from trying to minimize their own corporate tax bill to trying to minimize the total of all taxes paid on corporate income, based on the relative rates of personal tax on equity income and interest income. Miller (1977) argues that this means there will be an equilibrium level of corporate debt, but the equilibrium debt-equity ratio will therefore only apply to the corporate sector as a whole, not to individual firms. Investors will be attracted to a capital structure which is tax efficient for them, but they won't pay a premium for an individual firm to change its capital structure, as that premium would cancel out the savings that were made by tax efficiency. With a clientele of investors already attracted to their specific capital structure, and without a premium on offer it may not be worthwhile for a firm to change its capital structure, and therefore there may not be an optimal capital structure for an individual firm.

This section has shown that tax rates can have a notable influence on a firm's capital structure choice. Corporate tax can encourage a firm to take on more debt due to its tax-deductible status, while the addition of personal taxes on equity or interest income may suggest there is little to no benefit to taking on debt and no optimal capital structure. But while tax may play a role in capital structure choice, the biggest factor of all may be the presence of imperfections in capital markets. This is the focus of the next section.

2.5 Market Imperfections

Modigliani and Miller's theory that the method of financing is irrelevant and there is no optimal capital structure is based on the assumption of perfect capital markets. And therefore it follows that the presence of imperfections in capital markets can motivate a choice toward or away from debt, creating an optimal capital structure for a firm.

Two key requirements for perfect capital markets are for 'outsider' investors to have the same access to information as 'insiders' such as firm managers, and for the only sources of financing for a firm to be debt or equity. In practice however a firm can also rely on internal financing, the periodic firm income not distributed to shareholders. And as 'insider' firm managers, employees, or major shareholders will naturally know more about the amount of money their firm generates internally for internal financing than 'outsider' general investors, there is a problem of information asymmetry. Because of this asymmetry and lack of knowledge 'outsider' general investors may play it safe and assume a firm has less money available for internal financing than it actually does in reality, and assume a firm has greater operating risk with more uncertainty in its cash flows than it actually has. Due to this assumption of greater risk general 'outsider' investors may raise their required rate of return (the cost of capital) and issue less capital when a firm seeks external financing. The penalising effect of information asymmetry between firm insiders and outsiders is usually worse for the issue of equity than the issue of debt, with the former far more likely to have a negative effect on a firm's share price and value than the latter. One reason is because firms often take on debt from banks, which will have greater access to a firms' inner workings and cash flows than general 'outsider' investors, and will have greater control over their liquidity. A firm getting a loan from a bank gives 'outsider' investors reassurance that it can likely pay its bills, and shareholders. Issuing debt can suggest managers have confidence in the future, to pay it back. On the other hand the issue of new equity capital will not only reduce the relative influence of current shareholders in percentage terms, and their relative control over a firm's liquidity, but may also be seen as a desperate move to get money from the people who will know the least about a firm's internal financial position. Information asymmetry may therefore push firms toward debt over equity, to ensure there is an optimal capital structure. This is especially true for firms which general investors will know little about, such as small companies and new start-ups.

Pecking Order Theory (Myers and Majluf, 1984) states that when firms hold asymmetric information that investors don't firms will prefer to use internal financing first as a source of funding, adjusting the amount of earnings they pay out to shareholders as dividends based on the investment opportunities. When internal financing isn't available they'll turn to risk-free debt from bank loans, and if that method of borrowing isn't possible firms will then turn to debt via securities and issue bonds to investors. Only when firms have no other option will they turn to equity and issue new shares. This theory suggests a clear pecking order in funding, where firms prefer debt financing over equity.

Another assumption of perfect capital markets, and no optimal capital structure, is that firm managers act solely to benefit shareholders. In practice however managers may do a poor job of maximizing firm value for shareholders, instead focusing on vanity projects or just doing enough to keep their job and the associated benefits. But debt has the potential to control managers and ensure they act to benefit shareholders as they are meant to. The logic is that taking on greater debt increases the risk of a firm going bankrupt or facing severe financial difficulties, and if that happens firm managers and corporate executives may lose their jobs and generous benefits packages. Shareholders often prefer a firm to take on more debt than equity for this reason, and taking on greater debt puts greater pressure on firm management to do their jobs well, raising the firm's value for shareholders. Ofek (1993) backs up this idea with empirical evidence, and finds that firms with more leverage react faster to a financial crisis, with cuts in dividend payments, employee layoffs, and asset restructuring, to help their firm and increase its value.

This section has so far looked at the benefits of debt, but Trade-Off Theory states that there are both benefits and costs to taking on debt, and the two must be balanced out by a firm deciding its debt-equity mix. Taking on too much debt can push a firm to bankruptcy or into financial distress, as just noted, which will have significant costs for a firm that reduce its value. In this analysis the value of a firm can therefore be found with the following formula, where V_L is the market value of a levered (with debt) firm, V_U is the market value of an unlevered (no debt) firm, TS is the present value of the tax shield debt provides, and BFD is the present value of bankruptcy and financial distress costs:

$$V_L = V_U + TS - BFD$$

The value of a levered firm equals the value of an unlevered firm plus the present value of the tax savings offered by debt, minus the present value of bankruptcy and financial distress costs. When all corporate and investors personal taxes are included, along with direct and indirect bankruptcy and distress costs, it's possible that the two may cancel each other out. But there may be an optimal capital structure, with enough debt to generate tax savings, but not enough to see a firm face bankruptcy and financial distress costs. This optimal debt-equity ratio would theoretically occur when the present value of the tax savings from taking on additional debt equals the present value of financial distress and bankruptcy costs. In order to calculate the expected costs of bankruptcy or financial distress for a firm the following formula can be used, where BFD_C is the costs of financial distress or bankruptcy, and p is the probability of financial distress or bankruptcy occurring:

$$\text{Expected costs of financial distress} = p \times BFD_C$$

The probability of bankruptcy is the probability that a firm's cash flows are not enough to pay its debt obligations to creditors. This is a function of a firm's operating cash flow relative to its cash flow of debt, and the volatility of a firm's operating cash flow. One way to estimate a firm's probability of bankruptcy is to look at historical rates for firm insolvency (i.e. being unable to meet debt obligations) produced by major institutions, which will show firms' default rates for different credit ratings.

Another problem with taking on debt is the agency costs it brings with it, especially in times of financial distress. A clear principal-agent problem can occur, where a principal (i.e. the creditor) must rely on firm management (i.e. the agent) to act on their behalf, but the interests of agent and principal conflict. In times of financial trouble management may engage in 'risk-shifting', substituting assets to invest in high-risk projects, where if it is successful shareholders receive the benefit, but if it is not then creditors must pick up the bill. Underinvestment is also a problem, and management may ignore projects which offer a positive expected net present value, knowing that the returns would all be taken by creditors. Asset stripping is possible, and firms may sell assets-in-place or distribute high dividends to shareholders, to try and avoid losing their resources to creditors, even though this may harm the firm. In response to this, or the threat of it, creditors are likely to raise the required rate of return on debt, the cost of debt, as a firm's debt level increases and financial distress becomes more likely. Therefore one of the biggest drawbacks associated with a firm taking on debt is that it reduces the firm's financial flexibility, and its ability to issue more debt in the future. A study by Brounen et al. (2004) found that financial flexibility was the most important factor determining the amount of corporate debt held by European firms.

Overall, the presence of market imperfections suggests there is an optimal capital structure for a firm, with enough debt to make use of its benefits, but not enough to push a firm close to financial distress. Firms in corporate sectors with higher operating income and fixed assets can tolerate higher leverage, while firms in sectors with lower operating income and more intangible assets should have less.

3 Dividend Policy

3.1 Dividend Irrelevance Theory

Every firm must decide how much of its net cash flow to retain and reinvest, and what to pay out to shareholders as dividends. The two options both give value to shareholders; dividends by giving direct payments to them, and reinvestment by raising the value of the firm shareholders own. Retaining earnings and reinvesting them could be seen as a form of equity financing for future investment projects, while dividends require a firm to make constant payments much like debt involves. The debate over retaining earnings or paying them out as dividends can therefore be seen as an extension to the capital structure question, and just as Miller and Modigligani argued that in perfect capital markets capital structure is irrelevant to firm value, they also argue that dividend policy is irrelevant to firm value. The basic idea is the same as explained earlier with 'home-made leverage', and retained and reinvested earnings are thought to allow shareholders to create their own 'home-made dividends' from the increased value of their shares, achieving the same as a dividend at no extra cost by selling some shares.

Miller and Modigliani (1961) demonstrated the irrelevance of dividends in influencing firm value, and the equivalence of retaining earnings and paying them out, using the basic valuation model for a firm's share price:

$$P_0 = (D_1 + P_1) / (1 + k_E)$$

Where P_0 is the current share price, D_1 is the dividend in year 1, P_1 is the share price in year 1, and k_E is the cost of equity. A firm's market value equals its current share price, P_0, multiplied by the number of shares the firm has issued, N, and therefore firm value = NP_0. The valuation model for a firm's value, NP_0, is simply the basic valuation model for one share but with the share price in year 1, P_1, and dividend per share in year 1, D_1, each multiplied by the number of shares the firm has issued, N:

$$NP_0 = (ND_1 + NP_1) / (1 + k_E)$$

If NP_0 can be represented differently, without a term for future dividends, D_1, then it has been shown that firm value is not influenced by dividends, and therefore dividend policy is irrelevant to firm value. And the next few paragraphs will attempt to do that.

A firm is considering a new investment opportunity, I, to take place at the end of year 1. This investment opportunity would be funded using the firm's retained earnings, R_E, and money raised by issuing new shares. The number of new shares issued, S, multiplied by the price of each share at that time (the end of year 1), P_1, gives the total amount of money raised by issuing new shares, SP_1. Therefore the cost of this investment opportunity is:

$$I = R_E + SP_1$$

Rearranging this gives:

$$SP_1 = I - R_E$$

Retained earnings, R_E, are equal to total earnings, E, minus the amount of earnings paid out as dividends. Dividends paid out at the end of year 1 (when the investment would take place) are each worth D_1, while the number of existing shares issued which dividends would be paid on is N. The amount of earnings paid out as dividends is therefore ND_1, which means retained earnings, R_E, are:

$$R_E = E - ND_1$$

The money raised by issuing new shares is therefore:

$$SP_1 = I - (E - ND_1)$$
$$SP_1 = I - E + ND_1$$

This value needs to be added into the equation given earlier for the valuation of a firm's shares, NP_0, in order for the dividend term, D_1, to then be removed. The only way for this to be permissible however, and achieved without changing the equation, is for SP_1 to be both added and subtracted from the equation at the same time. The total value of a firm NP_0 was:

$$NP_0 = (ND_1 + NP_1) / (1 + k_E)$$

And the addition and subtraction of SP_1 from this equation gives:

$$NP_0 = (ND_1 + NP_1 + SP_1 - SP_1) / (1 + k_E)$$

Which can be rewritten as:

$$NP_0 = [ND_1 + (N + S)P_1 - SP_1] / (1 + k_E)$$

Now the value of SP_1, $SP_1 = I - E + ND_1$, can be entered into the equation in place of SP_1:

$$NP_0 = [ND_1 + (N + S)P_1 - (I - E + ND_1)] / (1 + k_E)$$
$$NP_0 = [ND_1 + (N + S)P_1 - I + E - ND_1] / (1 + k_E)$$
$$NP_0 = [(N + S)P_1 + E - I] / (1 + k_E)$$

This states the total value of a firm's shares, a firm's market value, is determined by the number of issued shares (N), the number of new shares that will be issued (S), the price of a share at the end of year 1 (P_1), the total earnings of the firm (E), the value of the investment opportunity under consideration (I), and the cost of equity (k_E). There is no term for dividends here, and therefore the value of a dividend has no effect on a firm's value. A dividend could be zero, or it could be one million, and it will make no difference. Based on this evidence it therefore doesn't matter whether a firm retains earnings or pays them out as dividends, and dividend policy is irrelevant to firm value. This analysis is all theoretical however, based on the assumption of perfect capital markets. The next section looks into why this assumption of perfect capital markets may not hold in the real world, and what may motivate firm management's dividend decisions in practice.

3.2 The Dividend Decision

While a firm's dividend policy may have no effect on its value in theory and in perfect capital markets, in practice markets contain imperfections, such as firm insiders knowing more about the current financial position of the firm than outsiders in the market. Dividends are therefore used as a means of communication between the firm and the wider financial market, and in this way they could affect a firm's perceived value and in turn their actual market value. A rise in the dividend paid to shareholders can signal the firm is profitable with strong earnings, while a dividend reduction may signal that earnings have fallen and a firm can't afford to pay out as much as it did. On the other hand a rise in the dividend may be interpreted negatively, and seen as a lack of investment opportunities for the firm, while a fall in the dividend may be seen as a strategy for renewed growth with new lucrative investment opportunities. A firm must therefore be careful with its dividend policy, or risk sending out the wrong signals to investors.

The two key features of a dividend policy are the payout ratio, and the rate of growth of dividends per share. The payout ratio is found with the following formula, where dividends and net income are for the same period:

Payout ratio = Total dividends / Net income

After a firm has decided on its payout ratio it can distribute dividends in different ways. An advance dividend sees a fraction of the upcoming annual dividend paid in advance ahead of time, and this is a way for a firm to smooth out cash outflows from the company and cash inflows to shareholders. A preferential dividend is a dividend paid before other regular dividends, and this is a way to reward loyal shareholders who have held shares for multiple years, and to assure them that in the event the firm is financially unable to pay dividends to all shareholders they will be sure to get theirs. A dividend can also be paid in shares, which allows a company to distribute earnings to shareholders without having to part with the corresponding cash funds, but it may involve limited redistribution of firm ownership.

A higher payout ratio is linked with lower stock price volatility, other things being equal. The high payout ratio suggests the stock behaves more like a bond, with regular payments, to reassure investors and make the stock price less volatile. High dividend payouts may be desirable for this reduction in stock price volatility, or as a source of current income for shareholders, or as a tool to communicate information to the market. Agency theory sees dividend payments as a way for management to defuse tensions between themselves and shareholders, the owners of the firm, caused by the principal-agent problem where shareholders (the principal) must rely on firm management (the agent) to act on their behalf. A higher dividend payout may keep shareholders happy and less likely to cause problems for management. On the other hand low dividend payouts may be desirable as stock option plans or capital gains can offer lower taxed alternatives for shareholders, and if transaction costs are low shareholders seeking cash may be able to just sell their shares for 'home-made dividends' at no extra cost.

If a firm's return on capital employed (ROCE) is greater than its weighted average cost of capital (WACC), then a company creates value by reinvesting its earnings, and shareholders may want the dividend payout to be low or even zero. And if a firm's ROCE is lower than its WACC then a company will destroy value by reinvesting its earnings, and shareholders may want all of the firm's earnings to be paid out as dividends. A firm may therefore want to tailor its dividend based on the relationship between its expected ROCE and its WACC. However, a dividend that varies frequently communicates no useful information to investors, and may suggest the firm's managers are incompetent and have no coherent business strategy. If investors come to believe this then the firm's market price and value can fall significantly. Therefore, even if earnings are cyclical, with a firm's ROCE alternating between being greater than WACC and less than WACC, a firm may still want to keep its dividend steady.

Koch and Sun (2004) find empirical evidence that when a firm changes its dividend investors are more likely to believe that past earnings changes are representative of future earnings levels. This may discourage firms from making changes in their dividend, as any unexpected fall in earnings could then be interpreted by investors as a sure sign of lower future earnings, which may lower the firm's market price and create a self-fulfilling downward spiral for the firm.

A firm's dividend policy may be able to affect a firm's value in imperfect markets, due to differential tax rates on dividends and other payment options, transaction costs preventing an investor creating costless 'home-made dividends', or due to the signalling effect dividends make to investors. But the existence of clienteles attracted to a specific dividend policy may limit the impact of this in practice. A firm may choose not to make changes to its dividend as it may cost them their current investors, a clientele who invested in the firm specifically as its payout policy was appropriate for their individual needs.

Lintner (1956) found that firms have dividend payout ratio targets based on expected future earnings, and managers are more focused on changes in dividends than on the absolute level of a dividend. Managers are thought to be reluctant to make dividend changes that may have to be reversed later, and try to avoid cutting dividends if possible. Changes in dividends follow shifts in long-run sustainable earnings, but managers attempt to keep changes in the dividend as small as possible following significant variations in earnings, preferring to stabilize dividends with gradual sustainable increases where possible. Brav et al. (2005) agree with Lintner that dividends are smoothed through time, and that increases in dividends follow shifts in long-run sustainable earnings, but their study almost 50 years after Lintner's finds that the link between earnings and dividends has weakened. In the 21st century many managers prefer share repurchases over issuing dividends, when long-run sustainable earnings allow it. Firm managers believe that share repurchases are a more flexible way to return money to shareholders than dividends, and they also come with several other potential benefits. Share repurchases are discussed in more detail in the next section.

3.3 Share Repurchases

Share repurchases, or stock buybacks, are where a company buys back its own shares and either keeps them on its balance sheet or cancels them. This is known as a capital reduction or a capital decrease and it reduces the quantity of shares in circulation by the number of shares bought back. When taxes are ignored, if a firm buys back shares from all shareholders in direct proportion to their relative holdings, then cancels those shares, the capital decrease which results is identical to the payment of a dividend. Money is transferred from the firm to its shareholders without any change in the ownership structure of the company.

A capital decrease involving a distribution of cash followed by a cancellation of shares can be achieved in a few different ways. If a company is publicly listed it can buy back stock in the open market. Alternatively, a firm can make a tender offer, a public offer of a share repurchase to shareholders. Or a company can reduce the par value of all shares, which automatically reduces the amount of authorized capital.

From an economic standpoint a capital reduction represents a reduction in a firm's equity capital. And a firm may have good reason to reduce its equity level if there is a lack of opportunities to invest in at the required rate of return. Theoretically, if a business has run out of investment opportunities which generate sufficient profits it shouldn't just pay out all of its earnings, it should also return some (or all) of its equity capital. From a tax standpoint a capital reduction is treated as a distribution of a firm's assets. And if the goal is to transfer cash from the company to its shareholders then buying back shares is a more tax efficient way to distribute excess capital than paying a dividend. Another reason a firm may seek to make a share repurchase is that it can signal good news to investors, driving up the firm's share price in the market, as the fact that a firm wants to buy back shares suggests they are undervalued. Stock buybacks can also be an efficient way to transfer value, between shareholders who refuse to sell their stock as they want to increase their stake in the company and gain more power, and shareholders who will agree to sell back their stock at a price exceeding its value. A share repurchase may also be used by a firm as a way to try to avoid paying its debts to creditors, as while a firm is legally obliged to give creditors payments on their debt before they pay dividends to shareholders, stock buybacks may be seen as a way around this, even though creditors can try to block it.

A repurchase of shares by a company will result in an increase in earnings per share (known as an EPS accretion) if E / P, annual earnings per share divided by price per share, exceeds the after-tax interest rate paid on incremental debt. But a repurchase of shares by a firm will result in a decrease in earnings per share (known as EPS dilution) if E / P is less than the rate of interest paid on incremental debt. A stock buyback will also increase the book value of equity per share, if the book value per share before the share repurchase is greater than the repurchase price per share. A share repurchase and capital decrease will not necessarily create value, as it doesn't reduce a firm's cost of capital. To create value a firm must buy back its shares at a price lower than they are truly worth. But a firm will avoid the destruction of value if it uses cash to buy back shares instead of investing cash in investments which will offer a return less than the cost of equity.

Whether a share repurchase creates value for an individual investor depends on how the shares were sold. If the capital decrease occurred with a public offer (a tender offer), or with a reduction of the par value of shares, then the difference between the investor's original acquisition price and the repurchase price they paid is considered a dividend, and is then taxed at the investor's marginal income tax rate. But if the shares were bought from an investor as part of a stock buyback action by the firm then the investor will pay a capital gains tax, as with a normal sale of shares. The increase in popularity of stock buybacks relative to dividends is largely connected to this last fact, and while firms may not necessarily have a preference between the two investors will prefer stock buybacks, if it sees them pay a lower capital gains tax rate and reduces their tax bill.

4 Option Theory

4.1 Options Contracts

Firms working with stocks and other securities are exposed to risk every day, and prices can change suddenly and significantly to potentially cost firms huge amounts of money. Financial derivatives help a firm to reduce the impact of this volatility and hedge risk, or alternatively can be used to try and profit from the volatility. Derivatives are products whose value derives from and is dependent upon the value of an underlying asset, but which include features to give greater flexibility to an investor.

Options contracts are a type of derivative that give the holder the right, but not the obligation, to buy or sell a security on or before a given date, at a fixed price (exercise price) agreed upon today. European options can only be exercised *on* the expiration or maturity date of the option, while American options can be exercised at any time *before* the expiration date of the option. The options are designated European or American based on the features of the option, and it has nothing to do with where in the world the options contract is traded. Basic and common 'vanilla' options are often traded in exchanges, organized markets with transparency and specific and detailed trading rules. Exotic options with more complex features are generally traded over the counter (OTC), in a two-way market between brokers and dealers with less transparency. Irrespective of the type, the defining feature of options is that there is no obligation for the holder to buy or sell, unlike with other derivatives such as forwards or futures. But this lack of obligation comes with a price, and buying an option position requires the upfront payment of a premium.

There are two main types of options; calls and puts. A call option gives buyers the right to buy the share at the exercise price, also known as the strike price, up to the date the options contract expires. The writer (seller) of the call option contract must sell shares of the underlying security to the buyer of the call option at the previously agreed price, if the buyer decides to exercise the option and 'call' for the shares. A put option gives buyers the right to sell the share at the exercise price, up to the date the options contract expires. The writer (seller) of the put option contract must buy shares of the underlying security from the buyer of the put option at the fixed exercise price, if the buyer decides to exercise the option and 'put' the shares to the writer. A buyer of an option has a 'long' position, whether the option involved is a call or a put, and must pay a premium to the seller or writer of an option who has a 'short' position.

The intrinsic value of an option depends upon the relationship between the underlying asset's current share price and the exercise price for the option, and whether the option is a call or a put. An option will have intrinsic value for a buyer, known as 'in-the-money', if:

> **Call:** Share price > Exercise price
> **Put:** Share price < Exercise price

An option will have no intrinsic value for a buyer, known as 'out-of-the-money', if:

> **Call:** Share price < Exercise price
> **Put:** Share price > Exercise price

And an option is 'at-the-money', also with no intrinsic value for a buyer, if:

> **Call:** Share price = Exercise price
> **Put:** Share price = Exercise price

Even if an option is 'in-the-money' with intrinsic value it may still not be profitable for a buyer, if the premium paid for it is greater than the difference between the share price and the exercise price. In order for a call option to be profitable for a buyer the share price must exceed the sum of the exercise price plus the premium. And in order for a put option to be profitable for a buyer the exercise price must be greater than the sum of the share price plus the premium. The situation for a writer (seller) of an option is the mirror image of that for the buyer. When a call option is profitable for a buyer (long call) it generates a loss for a seller (short call), and vice versa. And when a put option is profitable for a buyer (long put) it generates a loss for a seller (short put), and vice versa.

A series of diagrams can help to explain the profits associated with various different options. In this example a call option involves a premium of $5 that the buyer must pay to the seller for the option, while the exercise or strike price for the call option is $50. The first diagram shows the payoffs for the buyer of the call option, i.e. a long call, as the stock price of the underlying asset changes.

Long Call payoffs

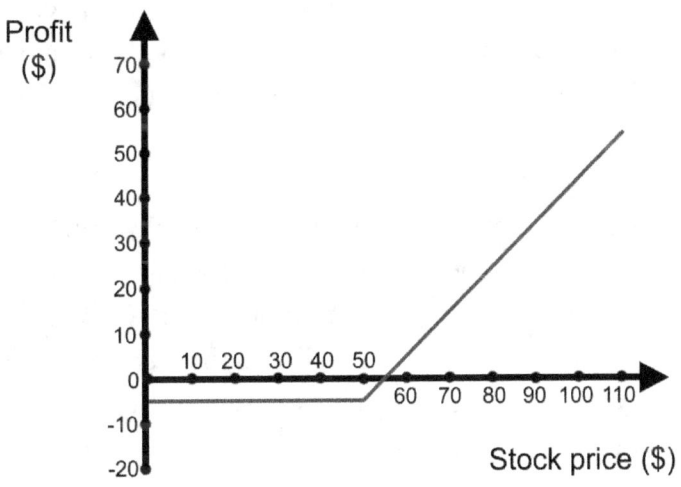

If the share price of the underlying asset is less than $50 the buyer will not exercise their right to 'call' for the shares at the previously agreed exercise price of $50, as there is no financial gain in doing so. The option will not be used, but the buyer will still be out of pocket by the premium they had to pay up front to buy the option, and will therefore have a negative profit (i.e. a loss) of – $5. This is shown in the diagram by the horizontal line from a $0 stock price to a $50 stock price, associated with a –$5 profit.

If the share price exceeds the exercise price the buyer of the call has a financial gain in exercising the option and can be expected to do so, if allowed. For a European option the share price must exceed the fixed exercise price at the option's maturity date, as that is the only time a European option can be exercised. But for an American option the share price could exceed the strike price at any time before the call option's expiration date, as that is when an American option can be exercised.

The upward sloping line in the long call payoffs diagram represents the situations where a buyer of a call will exercise the option, and the corresponding profits for a given stock price. With a share price of $52, for example, the buyer of the call can buy shares of the underlying asset at the option exercise price of $50. This would generate $2 and when the $5 premium paid for the option is subtracted the overall result is a negative profit of –$3. Still a loss, but less of a loss than if the option is not exercised. If the stock price is $80 then exercising the call and buying the asset at the $50 exercise price generates $30, and after the premium of $5 is subtracted the profit for the buyer is $25. And if the stock price was $110 then after the $50 exercise price and $5 premium to buy the option are subtracted the buyer of the call has a $55 profit.

The next diagram gives the payoffs for the seller of a call, i.e. a short call, and these are the exact mirror image of the payoffs for a call buyer in the last diagram. If the stock price is less than the exercise price of $50 the buyer of the call won't exercise it, and therefore the seller has a profit of $5, the premium that was paid for the option.

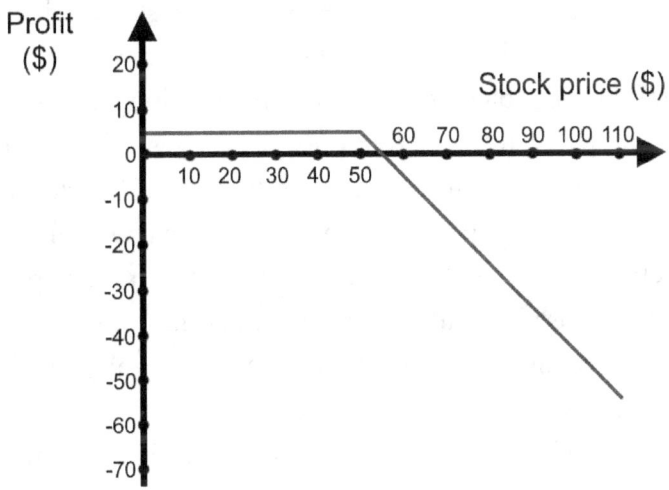

Short Call payoffs

But if the stock price of the underlying asset exceeds the $50 exercise price the buyer will exercise the call. The corresponding payoffs the seller of the call will receive for a given stock price are shown by the downward sloping line. If the share price is $52 the seller loses $2 when the call is exercised for $50, but they made a $5 premium when the call was sold so the overall seller profit is – $2 + $5 = $3, the mirror image of the – $3 loss for the buyer at a $52 share price. Similarly, an $80 stock price means $50 – $80 + $5 = –$25 loss for the seller. And a $110 share price gives $50 – $110 + $5 = –$55 seller loss. Buyer and seller payoffs are mirrored and one's profit is the other's loss, as their payoffs sum to zero.

The next two diagrams are for put options. In this example a put option involves a premium of $10 for a buyer to acquire it, while the exercise or strike price to activate the option is $100. This first diagram shows the payoffs for the buyer of a put option, i.e. a long put, as the share price of the underlying asset changes. If the share price is greater than the exercise price of $100 then the buyer of the put will not exercise the option and their right to sell, as there is no financial gain in doing so. The option will go unused but the buyer of the put has already paid the $10 premium to buy it, giving an overall negative profit, a loss, of –$10. This is shown by the horizontal line from a $100 stock price and above in the diagram. But if the stock price is below $100 then the buyer of the put option can improve their payoff, and can be expected to exercise the option and 'put' shares to the seller, for the $100 exercise price. The corresponding payoffs for the buyer of the put option, for a given share price, are represented by the downward sloping line in the diagram. If the stock price was $90, for example, the buyer of the put would generate $10 by selling at the exercise price, and when the premium they had already paid for the put was subtracted their overall profit would be $0. Better than the –$10 loss if they never exercise the put option. And if the share price was $30 the buyer of the put could make $70 selling the put at the $100 exercise price, and after the $10 premium is subtracted they would have a $60 profit.

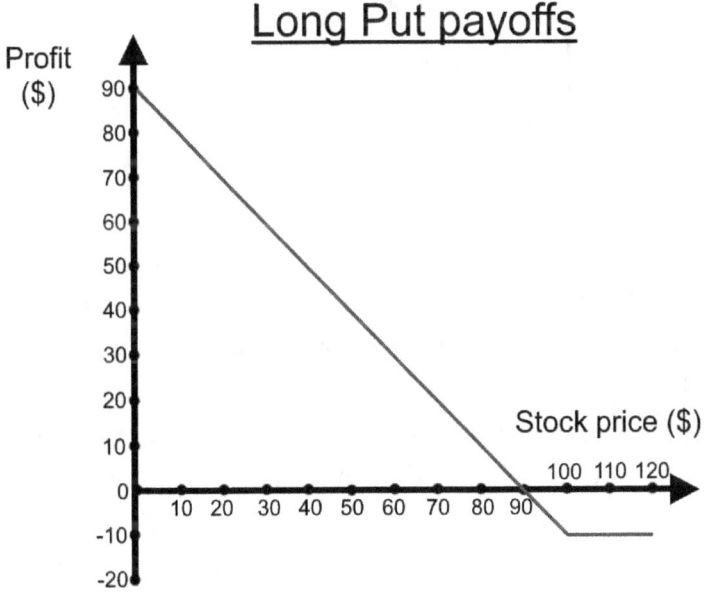

The payoffs for the seller of a put option, i.e. a short put, are the mirror image of those for the buyer of a put and a long put. They are shown in the next diagram.

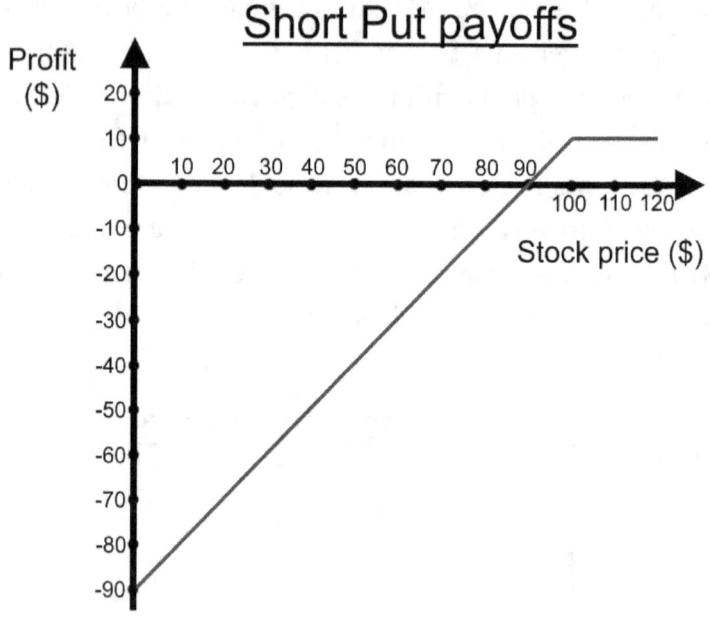

Short Put payoffs

If the share price of the underlying asset exceeds the $100 stock price the buyer won't exercise it, and the seller's profit is therefore the $10 premium they received for the sale of the option. But if the stock price is less than the $100 exercise price the buyer of the put will exercise it to improve their payoff, and this reduces the payoff of the seller of the put, as shown in the diagram by the upward sloping line. If the stock price is $90 the seller of the put loses $10 on the $100 exercise price, but when the $10 premium they made selling the put is added the overall profit for the put seller is $0. And if the share price is $30 the seller of the put loses $70 on the $100 exercise price, and when the $10 premium is added their overall loss is – $60, the mirror image of what the buyer of a put makes in profit for a $30 stock price.

An investor will buy a call option (long call) if they expect that the price of the underlying security will rise. This allows the buyer to profit from the rising security price without having to commit large amounts of money to the transaction, in case the price doesn't actually rise or their money is needed elsewhere. Writers of call options (short call) usually sell calls on shares they already possess, as they expect that the share price will either fall or stay stable. As long as the share price is not expected to rise then the buyer can be relied upon to not exercise the call option, and the seller of the call profits by the size of the premium they received for the option.

Investors buy put options (long put) if they expect the price of the underlying security to fall. An investor may already own shares of the underlying security and buy the put to hedge against the possibility of the price falling, to ensure they don't suffer a loss and can sell at a higher and previously agreed exercise price. The writer of a put (short put) expects the price of the underlying security to rise or remain stable. They therefore expect to profit by the size of the premium the buyer paid for it, and count on the buyer not facing a declining share price and exercising their right to sell at a higher exercise price, to cost the put writer money.

Writing a call or buying a put is a way for the holder of the underlying security to reduce their risk exposure at a price they find acceptable. Buying a call or writing a put is the opposite, a way for an investor to take on additional risk exposure in return for a chance of increased gains. Options markets therefore perform an important role, redistributing the risk associated with an investment and balancing out the gains and losses caused by potential price movements.

4.2 Black-Scholes Option Pricing Model

In 1973 Black, Scholes, and Merton developed a formula to value European call options (c), on a non-dividend paying stock, assuming no transaction costs. Determining factors are the underlying security's current share price (S_0), the exercise price (X), the continuously compounded annual risk-free rate (r), time in years till the option's maturity (T), and the share price's volatility (σ). N() is the cumulative probability distribution for a variable with a standard normal distribution, with 0 mean and 1 standard deviation:

$$c = S_0 N(d_1) - Xe^{-rT} N(d_2)$$

Where (d_1) and (d_2) are determined by:

$$d_1 = [\ln(S_0/X) + (r + \sigma^2/2)T] / \sigma T^{0.5}$$
$$d_2 = d_1 - \sigma T^{0.5}$$

In order to calculate the value of a call the value of d_1 would first be calculated, then the value of d_2. With these the corresponding value for d_1 in a standard normal probability distribution table gives $N(d_1)$ for the Black-Scholes equation, while the corresponding table value for d_2 gives the value of $N(d_2)$ to use.

The five factors thought to determine the price of a European call option affect the price in different ways. A rise in the current share price (S_0) will result in an increase in the price of the call. If already in-the-money this will move the call option further into it with greater intrinsic value, but if not already in-the-money then it will be nearer to it, and more likely to be in it in the remaining time until the option expires. An option price's responsiveness to a change in the underlying asset's share price is known as the option delta.

The higher the exercise price (X) the lower the price and value of the call option, as a higher exercise price moves the call out-of-the-money or closer to being out-of-the-money. The greater the amount of time to maturity (T) of the option the greater the value and price of the call option, as there is more time for the share price of the underlying security to move in a way favourable to the option's holder.

An increase in the underlying asset's share price volatility (σ) will increase the price of the call, as greater volatility means a greater likelihood of large price movements that will generate a profit for the holder of a call. A rise in the risk-free rate of interest (r) will increase the price and value of a call. This means a greater discount rate and lowers the present value of the exercise price, meaning the stock price is more likely to exceed it to see the call in-the-money.

While the Black-Scholes formula is for valuing European call options on a non-dividend paying stock, it can also in theory be used to value American call options on a non-dividend stock too. This is because there is no logical reason to exercise an American call without dividends early, thereby essentially making it exactly the same and with the same value as a European call that will only ever be exercised at maturity. First, paying the exercise price on an American call early costs the call holder interest that could have been earned on that money. Second, holding onto the American call gives insurance against the share price falling below the exercise price. Third, no income is lost by waiting until the option's maturity to exercise the American call.

The value of a European put (p) on a non-dividend paying stock can also be determined. d_1 and d_2 are the same as for a call option, while the main equation for the price of a put is the mirror of that for a call:

$$p = Xe^{-rT}N(-d_2) - S_0N(-d_1)$$

$$d_1 = [\ln(S_0 / X) + (r + \sigma^2 / 2)T] / \sigma T^{0.5}$$
$$d_2 = d_1 - \sigma T^{0.5}$$

In terms of how the five factors affect the price and value of a put option, an increase in the volatility (σ) of the underlying asset's share price increases a put's price and value just as with a call option for the same reason. Greater volatility in prices increases the likelihood of movements that will profit the put holder. A greater time to maturity (T) will also raise the price of a put, as with a call, as there is more time for the share price to move in a way favourable to the put holder. The other three factors affecting a put operate in the opposite way to a call. The higher the exercise price (X) the higher the value of a put, as this moves a put closer to being or further in-the-money. The higher the stock price (S_0) the lower the price and value of a put option, as this moves the put out-of-the-money or closer to it. And a rise in the risk-free rate of interest (r) will reduce the value of a put, as it discounts the exercise price to a greater extent and makes it more likely that it will be below the stock price to push the put out-of-the-money.

4.3 Options Strategies

Traders can use options in different ways to suit their specific goals. Speculators hope to make money in financial markets by betting on the direction of prices, and different options can be combined to help them achieve this goal. For example, a speculator may expect that a firm is about to face a takeover, and predict that its share price will change significantly. However, the speculator may not know if the market will see the takeover favourably, pushing the firm's stock price up, or unfavourably, pushing the stock price down. Combining two options can help the speculator, and buying both a call (long call) and a put (long put) at the same exercise price will create a 'long straddle', with large price increases and large price decreases both generating profits.

In the following diagram the dotted line represents the payoffs associated with buying a call, shown by a line that is at first horizontal then upward sloping. And the dashed line represents the payoffs associated with buying a put at exactly the same exercise price, shown by a line that is at first downward sloping and then horizontal. With the two combined the payoffs are shown by the thicker unbroken line in a V shape. If the price stays close to the exercise price then the investor will have a profit below zero and suffer a loss. But if there is a large movement in the share price one way or another away from the exercise price, as the investor expecting a takeover predicts there will be, then the speculative investor will be able to enjoy a large and positive profit.

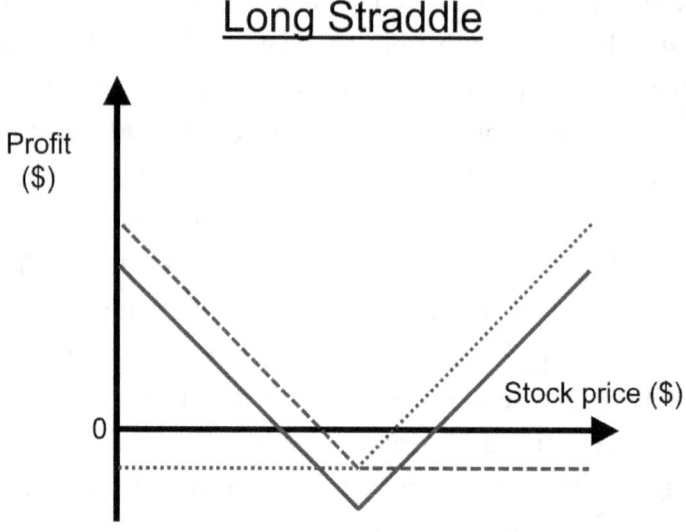

Long Straddle

Options can also be used by traders seeking to avoid the risk associated with price movements, known as hedgers. An investor may own stock and seek to benefit from potential stock price rises, but also want to ensure that they are protected in the event that the stock price falls. The solution is to combine the stock with an option, and buy a put. This 'protective put' will ensure that no matter how low the price falls the investor never loses more than the option's premium. The dotted line in the following diagram represents the payoffs associated with the investor's stock as its price changes, while the dashed line represents the payoffs associated with a long put. Combining the two gives the thicker unbroken line's payoffs, revealing the hedger loses no more than their put's premium at lower stock price levels, but can still profit from higher stock price levels.

Protective Put

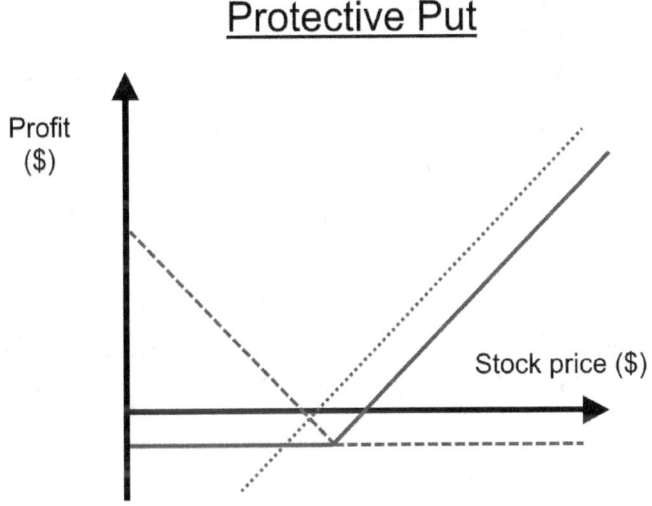

Finally, traders who seek to make riskless profits by getting involved with two or more transactions in different markets can also benefit from using options. Arbitrageurs simply need to compare the actual price of a call or put to what it is worth, and if the call or put's actual premium is lower than its value then there is an arbitrage opportunity.

A European call can only be exercised at maturity, and at maturity an investor will compare the stock price at that time to the exercise price they agreed earlier. The investor's profit (or loss) will be the stock price at that time (S_T) minus the exercise price they will pay (X), and that is what the call is worth to them. This all occurs at the European call's maturity however, and in order to find an arbitrage opportunity an arbitrageur must deal with prices in the present. The current stock price (S_0) is already a present value, but the exercise price which would only be paid at maturity (X) must be turned into a present value, and this is done using a compound interest formula in reverse. Multiplying by e^{-rT} finds the present value of the exercise price to be paid in the future at the option's maturity. Therefore an arbitrageur must subtract Xe^{-rT} from S_0 to find what the call is worth to them, and if the call premium price is lower than this there is an arbitrage opportunity.

For example, the current stock price (S_0) may be $30, the exercise price (X) on a European call paying no dividends may be $26, the time till the option's maturity (T) is six months and therefore T = 0.5, the risk-free rate (r) is 7% or 0.07, and the price of the call (c) may be $4. To determine if there is an arbitrage opportunity Xe^{-rT} must be calculated. $Xe^{-rT} = 26e^{-0.07 \times 0.5} = 26e^{-0.035} = \$25.11$. The call's worth to the investor is $S_0 - Xe^{-rT} = \$30 - \$25.11 = \$4.89$. And as this is greater than the call's buy price of $4, there is an arbitrage opportunity for the arbitrageur to exploit. The arbitrageur that owns the stock could sell it at its current stock price, $S_0 = \$30$, and then buy the undervalued call at $c = \$4$. This gives $\$30 - \$4 = \$26$ profit in the present. This can then be invested for risk-free interest for the six month life of the option until it reaches maturity, to generate $26e^{rT} = 26e^{0.035} = \$26.93$. If the stock price is greater than the \$26 exercise price by the time the European call has matured then the arbitrageur can exercise it for \$26, to end up with a riskless profit of $\$26.93 - \$26 = \$0.93$, and the stock he started with. And if the stock price has fallen below \$26, to \$25 for example, then greater profits are available. The arbitrageur can buy the stock for \$25, for riskless profits of $\$26.93 - \$25 = \$1.93$.

European puts can also be used by arbitrageurs to make riskless profits, if the price of the put is found to be lower than its worth, $Xe^{-rT} - S_0$. For example, the stock price (S_0) is \$40, exercise price (X) is \$49, time to maturity (T) is one year, risk-free rate (r) is 5% or 0.05, and the price of the put (p) is \$5. The value of the exercise price in the present is then, $Xe^{-rT} = 49e^{-0.05} = \$46.61$. The value of the put to the investor is therefore $Xe^{-rT} - S_0 = \$46.61 - \$40 = \$6.61$, which is greater than the price of the put at \$5, so there is therefore an arbitrage opportunity. The arbitrageur could borrow \$45 to buy both the stock (\$40) and the under-priced put option (\$5). By the time the put reaches maturity the investor would owe interest on the \$45 they borrowed, and the total amount of debt owed is

$45e^{rT} = 45e^{0.05} = \$47.31$. But if the stock price at that time is less than the exercise price of $49 the arbitrageur could exercise the put, and sell the stock at $49 for riskless profit of $49 − $47.31 = $1.69. And if the stock price is greater than the exercise price, at $50 for example, then the arbitrageur can sell their stock at that price for greater riskless profits of $50 − $47.31 = $2.69.

If a call or put's price deviates from the value it gives to investors then arbitrageurs will step in to exploit this for risk-free profits, until all profits have been arbitraged away and the market prices the call or put correctly. Arbitrage therefore plays an important role in keeping financial markets efficient, and call and put options priced correctly. Stoll (1969) put forward the idea of a put-call parity, which states that there will be a certain relationship between a European call at one exercise price and expiration date, and a European put at the same exercise price and expiration date. And if there is a divergence from this relationship and put-call parity then arbitrageurs will intervene for riskless profits, until put-call parity is naturally restored.

5 Mergers and Acquisitions

5.1 Merger Basics

Mergers and Acquisitions, or M&A for short, is the corporate strategy and management field relating to the merging with and acquiring of different companies. Firms use mergers or acquisitions as a tool to expand or improve their business, and increase their profits. The two terms are most often used interchangeably, and will be here, and both represent two or more companies combining together as one. But at times the term merger may be preferred to represent two firms of similar power coming together and combining resources willingly, while the term acquisition or takeover may be preferred if one firm has more power than the other and seeks to absorb it, perhaps against the will of some groups at the firm to be absorbed.

There are three different types of merger or acquisition. A horizontal merger is between two or more firms which operate in the same business area, for example two supermarkets. A vertical merger is between two or more companies in the same business area but different stages of the production chain, for example between a company that makes car parts, and a company that combines all car parts together to create a functioning vehicle to sell to the public. Finally, a conglomerate merger is a merger between firms involved in unrelated business activities. For example a merger between firms selling different products to increase the product line of each firm, or between companies operating in different and separate geographical areas to expand each company's geographical market reach.

Historically, mergers and acquisitions tend to come in waves, and greater merger activity often correlates with a bull market with rising share prices, and higher price-to-earnings ratios for firms. Shleifer and Vishny (2003) attempt to explain merger waves by arguing that at any given time in a given market there will be both overvalued firms and undervalued firms. In a bull market with rising share prices an overvalued company, whose share price has risen too far relative to its true value, will bid to acquire an undervalued company, whose share price hasn't risen enough given its true value and the market conditions it operates in. The bid will reduce the valuation and share price of the overvalued acquiring company, but the share price and firm value won't fall too quickly or too much (as it should), as when investors come to realize the overvalued firm is actually overvalued they'll also notice the acquired firm was undervalued, to keep the share price up. Mergers are therefore a way for a temporarily overvalued firm to profit from their overvaluation, securing a permanent gain to their share price and firm value before the market eventually adjusts to their true value.

Another reason mergers and acquisitions often come in waves, during bull markets when firms do well on average with rising share prices, is because this is when firms have the most money to be able to fund a merger or acquisition. Only once firms have the required resources can they attempt to undertake the merger they want. The next section looks at the range of factors which can motivate a firm to want a merger, beyond overvalued firms acquiring undervalued firms as just mentioned.

5.2 Merger Motivations

One of the most common motivations for a merger is the belief that synergies will be created, and the two firms combined together will be greater than the sum of their parts. Economies of scale are often associated with mergers, where the two firms merged create a larger firm which may be able to lower its unit costs based on its greater size or operating scale. This can happen by the new firm making use of excess capacity, for example the one post-merger firm may be able to function with one large factory, while the two pre-merger firms used one each. Or alternatively the unit cost may be lowered by virtue of the merged firm spreading its fixed costs over more units, as its operating scale and production volume increases. A merger is often particularly associated with economies of scale in administrative costs, and research and development.

Another synergy linked with mergers are economies of scope, where two merging firms producing different but complementary goods combine to fill their missing pieces and lower their average cost. For example, a geographic economy of scope can see two merging companies in different countries each benefit from operating in a new region. Alternatively, two companies offering different types of financial services products could achieve economies of scope after a merger, by forming one firm with a full range of financial services for customers.

Economies of vertical integration are possible after a vertical merger, where two firms in the same business field but at different levels of the supply chain merge and lower costs. With the firm higher up the production chain essentially owning the suppliers they may be able to negotiate a better deal for lower costs, or even get supplied at the supplier's cost price. However, over integration between a supplier and another firm can cause the opposite effect and actually raise costs, for diseconomies of vertical integration. This may occur if after the merger the supplying firm no longer operates as efficiently, perhaps due to the influence of the other firm ruining its effective work practices.

A firm operating in a mature industry, where the growth phase for firms has passed and there are very few if any profitable investment opportunities left for firms, may have a large amount of surplus funds lying around and going to waste. And in this circumstance they may be motivated to consider an acquisition of another firm to make use of the funds in a way which can generate potential profits.

Potential efficiency gains can often motivate mergers, and two similar firms that merge can cut back on parts of their business which were identical and eliminate duplication to greatly reduce costs. Management of the new combined firm could keep the more effective aspects of each of the two businesses and discard the less successful duplicate, to increase sales, revenue, and profits.

If an industry is overcrowded with too many firms and too much output relative to what consumers actually want, then mergers may be an effective way to conduct industry consolidation. In order to avoid going bankrupt in a tough industry, several firms may merge together and then cut back on their overall production as one firm, efficiently removing duplicated areas of their operations, to improve their industry and the firm's own prospects.

The goal of market power and monopoly gains is often a motivating factor for mergers. Two rival firms in the same industry that merge with or acquire the other will have a far greater market share and more market power than when they were separate companies, and this can greatly increase company revenue and profits. They will have both a higher operating volume and greater influence in their industry, which can allow them to secure lower costs with suppliers. The two rival firms merging will also instantly reduce industry competition, of each other, removing their need to lower prices to outcompete each other to gain customers, thereby generating greater firm profits.

Firms may seek mergers or acquisitions to gain expertise in a certain area that they currently lack in their own firm, to help them compete more effectively in their industry. For example, a large video games producer may seek a merger with a much smaller games firm known for creating critically acclaimed video games. This benefits the larger firm by the acquisition of a talented team of game developers, while the smaller firm benefits from access to greater resources.

Growth is a leading motivating factor for mergers and acquisitions. A merger allows firms to grow much more quickly than they would naturally, although the growth is riskier as mergers may not necessarily work out as planned. This fast growth and greater resources can facilitate overseas expansion into new markets, allowing a firm to build up a customer base before smaller firms with less growth have amassed the resources to compete. Mergers can therefore create a first mover advantage for a firm, allowing them to act first in areas of the economy where speed can be a major advantage. Mergers can also potentially create earnings growth for a firm, where the earnings per share of the new company is greater than the earnings per share of either of the two individual firms before the merger occurred.

Firms created and managed by one individual may face problems of succession as the founding owner comes to the end of their life. In some cases a family member may be prepared to take over the leading management role to continue the family legacy, but if this isn't possible the firm may be sold and acquired by or merged with another firm.

Companies may be targeted for acquisition because they have a lower price to earnings ratio (P/E ratio) than the acquiring company, even if this is only because the target has fewer shares to pay earnings on and can therefore pay more earnings per share. A firm that acquires another with a higher earnings per share (EPS) will automatically increase its own EPS post-merger, and this is known as the 'bootstrap game'. However, this is only a short-term benefit as after the merger is completed the acquiring firm's growth in earnings per share (EPS) will be slower than pre-merger, due to share dilution caused by the acquired firm's influence. The following diagram shows the idea.

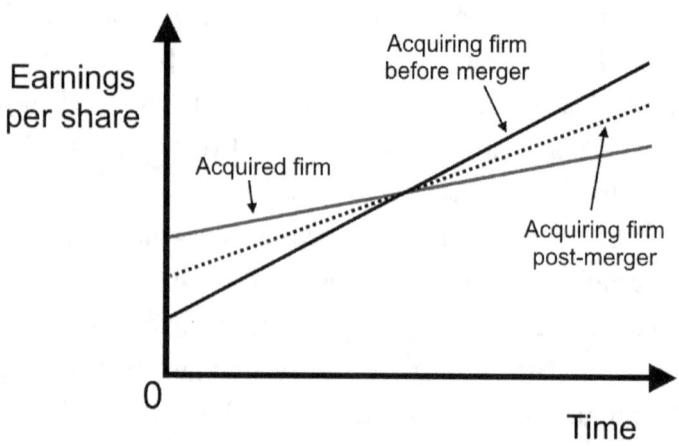

The acquired firm represented by the paler unbroken line has a higher EPS but slower EPS growth, while the acquiring firm represented by the darker unbroken line has a lower EPS but faster EPS growth. Combining the two firms in a merger results in a post-merger acquiring firm with earnings per share and EPS growth between that of the two firms, represented by the dotted line. At first in the short-term this new post-merger acquiring firm enjoys greater earnings per share than the acquiring firm was on track to make before the merger. But in the long-term due to share dilution this relationship reverses, and the post-merger firm is performing worse than it would have done if it hadn't made the acquisition.

Finally, the desire for diversification may be a factor motivating firms to consider a merger, and a merger is a quick way for a firm to increase the range of products or the number of sectors it operates in. Diversification can be appealing for firms as it reduces a firm's diversifiable risk, and if the product or sector the firm was originally involved with fails due to product specific or sector specific issues, the firm will be able to rely on unrelated products or sectors added post-merger which weren't affected. Diversification can also allow a firm to take on more debt financing if the acquired firm had a low debt level, or debt at a lower cost of debt than its own if the acquired firm was in a sector associated with lower risk. However, undertaking a merger or acquisition solely for greater diversification gains may not be the best idea, as a firm could diversify itself without one.

5.3 Merger Methods and Takeover Tactics

Firms interested in acquiring a publicly listed company often begin by building a stake in that company. This can be achieved by buying shares on the open market. Regulations vary by country, but in order to prevent a firm from acquiring another quietly and gradually without other shareholders realizing it, investors are typically required to publicly declare when they pass various percentage ownership thresholds in a company. This allows other minority shareholders to monitor and react to stake-building by other investors.

In many countries an investor or firm which has acquired a certain threshold of percentage ownership in a public company must make a mandatory offer to all other shareholders to buy back their shares, to take full control of the company. If a firm hasn't met the threshold of ownership to activate this rule then it must make a voluntary offer to attempt to takeover or merge with a firm. First a firm will attempt to determine how much the target is worth, which involves quantifying the value they expect to add as a result of the merger and then discounting it at the appropriate discount rate, before the firm makes an offer.

To improve their chances of success a firm's management may want to talk with the management of their target firm before they attempt a merger, in order to negotiate terms. If the negotiations succeed then the management of the target firm will recommend that their shareholders accept the offer, and a friendly merger can proceed. However, even if the merger is friendly one of the two management teams is likely to end up on top of the new merged firm, while the other loses out. If negotiations between the two firms' management teams don't succeed, or if a firm wants to bypass the other management team entirely for whatever reason, then they may still attempt a hostile takeover of their target. This is where a firm's management goes directly to their target firm's shareholders, the actual owners of a firm, to attempt to gain support for the merger / takeover, whether their management want it or not. The firm attempting the purchase may try to gain support at the next annual shareholders meeting, before they make a tender offer to the shareholders, a direct public offer to purchase a large amount of shares for a specified price.

After a tender offer to acquire a controlling share of a company has been publicly made the target's stock price will become more volatile, as market investors speculate whether or not the takeover will be successful. There are a number of tactics that a targeted firm's management can use to defend themselves from a takeover, and ensure it is unsuccessful. 'Shark Repellent' is where a firm's management makes changes to its company charter to try and obstruct a takeover. A 'Poison Pill' is an attempt by a firm's management to make their shares less useful to an acquiring firm. For example, a 'flip-in' is where a firm allows its shareholders, excluding an acquirer, to purchase additional shares at a discounted and attractive price. Existing shareholders will almost certainly purchase the additional shares as it means instant profits, and this dilutes the number of shares held by the acquiring firm, making the takeover more expensive and difficult to achieve. A 'flip-over' allows shareholders to purchase the acquirers shares at a discounted rate, such as two for one, after the merger in the future. This reduces the value of the acquirer's shares and means they will instantly lose money should they proceed with the acquisition, making it an effective way to dissuade takeovers.

Another strategy a firm may use to prevent a takeover is to require a supermajority to approve it before it can proceed. Instead of the usual majority, 50% or more, a firm may demand much more, for example an 80% approval rate, or it can't go ahead. Similarly, a firm may defend itself from a hostile takeover by putting a supermajority requirement on removing firm directors, making it more difficult for an acquiring firm to convince shareholders to remove firm management and replace them with 'yes men' who will approve the takeover. A firm may also take on large amounts of debt to scare off a takeover, as a firm that successfully acquires it would have to eventually pay all of its debt and face the associated risk. Finally, if a firm feels it can't stop a takeover by an unwanted firm it can seek a 'White Knight'. This is where a firm markets itself to another firm that it considers friendlier and more likely to act in its best interests, and actively courts an acquisition from them instead of the unwelcome suitor.

When a public offer is made for a company market regulation requires that it must be fully funded, and shareholders have an actual opportunity to sell their shares. This is because an offer made and then withdrawn soon after, as an unfunded offer may be, or where the potential buyer may fail to amass the funds required for financing should an offer be approved, as a partially funded offer could be, would cause disruption to the market.

The offer to merge with or acquire a firm can be funded with 100% cash, 100% shares, or some combination of both cash and shares. If cash alone is used then the acquiring company's shareholders face all of the business risk of the transaction, and should the acquired firm turn out to be overvalued then the acquired firm's shareholders face that decline in valuation. The benefits of using cash to fund a merger or acquisition is that it may be more appealing to the target firm's shareholders, thereby potentially making the merger more likely to be approved.

If only shares are used to fund a merger between two firms the transaction is known as an all-share merger, and there are three different types of all-share transactions between firms. A legal merger is where two or more firms are combined to form one single firm, with one of the firms usually dissolved and absorbed into the other. A contribution of shares merger is where the shareholders' of one of the merging companies (firm A) exchange their shares in return for the shares of the other merging company (firm B). The two companies still exist, with firm A as a subsidiary of firm B, and firm A's shareholders now shareholders of firm B. An asset contribution merger is where one of the merging companies (firm A) contributes some of its assets and liabilities to the other merging company (firm B) in return for shares issued by the latter company (firm B).

In an all-share funded merger the business risk of the transaction is shared between the two groups of shareholders. This is why stock is often preferred over cash to finance an acquisition if there's a chance the target may not be valued correctly. The acquiring firm's shareholders will also see their shareholders' equity increased by the value of the acquired firm's shareholders' equity in an all-share transaction, unlike a cash funded acquisition where the acquiring firm's shareholders' equity doesn't rise. Another advantage to paying in shares is that it removes the need to raise the cash, and without this obstacle a firm could merge with anyone they want, even very large companies with a high value. Paying in shares can also be a tool used to change firm ownership, and may be a tactic to dilute the stake held by an unpopular shareholder, or form a strong block of core shareholders.

In any attempted acquisition the target company must first be fully valued to determine a reasonable offer, but in an all-share funded acquisition the acquiring company must also be fully valued, since it will issue new shares to their target firm's shareholders. These valuations are normally done for the firms independent of any synergies expected from the merger, which will be valued separately. Both merging firms must of course agree on firm valuations before a merger can go ahead, and if one side feels it is being undervalued it is unlikely to proceed with the deal. The ratio of the two different merging firms' shareholders' equity values is known as the relative value. This relative value will determine how much of the new merged company will be owned by each of the former firms, and therefore the power and influence each set of shareholders hold in the new firm.

For example, there may be two companies, company A and company B, with the former planning an acquisition of the latter. They have both agreed on valuations of the respective shareholders' equity values, with company A's shareholders' equity valued at $480 million and company B's shareholders' equity valued at $300 million. The relative value for the company to be acquired, company B, is 300/480 = 0.625, and company B is worth 0.625 times the value of company A. With this relative value the relative ownership of each companies' shareholders in the new post-merger firm can be found. The relative ownership of company A in the new merged firm is equal to the share of value their company represents of the total value of the two firms:

$$V_A / (V_A + V_B)$$

Where V_A is the value of firm A's shareholders' equity, and V_B is the value of firm B's shareholders' equity. But as the relative value between the two firms is known these can be used in place of V_A and V_B, where V_A is replaced by 1 to represent firm A's value relative to firm A, and V_B is replaced by $V_B / V_A = 0.625$, to represent firm B's value relative to firm A:

$$V_A / (V_A + V_B) = 1 / [1 + (V_B / V_A)]$$
$$= 1 / [1 + (0.625)]$$
$$= 0.615 \text{ or } 61.5\%$$

The relative ownership of company A and its shareholders in the new post-merger firm is 61.5% of the new firm. Company B's relative ownership in the new merged firm is equal to:

$$V_B / (V_A + V_B)$$

And these values can again be replaced with relative values as was done for company A, where V_A is again replaced by 1, and V_B is replaced by $V_B / V_A = 0.625$ for reasons just explained:

$$V_B / (V_A + V_B) = (V_B / V_A) / [1 + (V_B / V_A)]$$
$$= 0.625 / [1 + (0.625)]$$

$$= 0.385 \text{ or } 38.5\%$$

The relative ownership of company B and its shareholders in the new post-merger firm is 38.5% of the new firm. This totals to 100% with company A's relative share of 61.5%, to account for all of the firm's ownership.

After relative value ratios for merging firms have been found the exchange ratio of shares follows as a direct result. This is the ratio of the number of shares of company A that will be given out in return for every one share of company B that is received in the all-share transaction. The formula for the exchange ratio is:

Exchange ratio (A for 1 B) = Relative value x (A_S / B_S)

Where A_S is the total number of shares that company A had issued before the merger, and B_S is the total number of shares that company B had before the merger. Note that while the exchange ratio is the number of shares of company A for 1 of company B, the relative value is the value of company B expressed as a ratio of company A's value.

The relative value ratio is the factor determining the exchange ratio of shares, and the relative ownership levels for each firm post-merger, in an all-share merger or acquisition. If the relative value ratio used in the merger is greater than the relative values of other financial metrics between the merging firms, such as net income or book value for example, then a firm will enjoy an accretion in value with respect to that financial metric. But if the relative value ratio used in the merger is less than the relative values of other financial metrics between the merging firms, then a firm will suffer a dilution in value with respect to that financial metric. The relative value agreed on between merging firms may deliberately be set to give an advantage and accretion in value to the firm being acquired, in order for the target firm's shareholders to agree to the deal. For example, when the relative value is being decided a premium may be added to the market value of the firm to be acquired. The premium would need to be high enough to motivate the target firm's shareholders to go ahead, but lower than the value of the synergy gains the acquiring firm expects to receive from the merger. The synergy gains and overall impact of mergers are discussed in depth in the next section.

5.4 The Value Impact of Mergers

The goal of a merger is to increase firm value, and therefore the present value of the post-merger new firm should exceed the total of the two firms before the merger:

$$PV_{AB} > PV_A + PV_B$$

Where PV_{AB} is the present value (PV) of post-merger new combined firm AB, PV_A is the present value of firm A before the merger, and PV_B is the present value of firm B before the merger. In order to calculate whether or not the present value of the new post-merger firm exceeds the present value of the two individual firms pre-merger, the gains and losses associated with the merger must be determined. The economic gain from the merger is the net cash flows from merger synergies divided by the relevant discount rate (i.e. the cost of capital). Merger gains are therefore the present value of the increased earnings arising from the merger, which can be found by subtracting the present value of the post-merger firm from the present value of the two pre-merger firms added together:

$$\text{Merger Gains} = PV_{AB} - (PV_A + PV_B)$$

The losses associated with the merger all relate to the difference between how much the acquiring firm (firm A) paid for its target (firm B) relative to the target's actual worth.

$$\text{Merger Losses} = \text{Acquisition Price} - PV_B$$

Taking the merger losses from the gains gives the net present value (NPV) of the merger:

$$NPV = \text{Merger Gains} - \text{Merger Losses}$$
$$NPV = PV_{AB} - (PV_A + PV_B) - (\text{Acquisition price} - PV_B)$$
$$NPV = PV_{AB} - PV_A - PV_B - \text{Acquisition price} + PV_B$$
$$NPV = PV_{AB} - PV_A - \text{Acquisition price}$$

The merger is worthwhile, with a positive net present value, if the merged firm (AB) is worth more than the value of the pre-merger acquiring firm (A) and the acquisition price combined. In other words, the acquisition price must be less than the value added by the acquired firm, and merger synergies. The following formula can be used to determine the minimum level of synergies required from a merger, to decide if a deal makes sense at the stock price:

$$(\text{Pre-merger total value of firms} + \text{synergy}) / \text{Post-merger no. shares} = \text{Pre-merger stock price}$$

The synergy values that a firm uses to decide on an acquisition and the price it pays will only be an estimate however, as no firm knows for sure whether or not expected merger synergies will actually materialize as planned. And empirical evidence shows that many forecast merger synergies never come to be, and mergers may turn out to be disappointing. Agrawal et al. (1992) finds that the shareholders of acquiring firms suffer a statistically significant loss of roughly 10% over the five year post-merger period. A more recent study by Giannopoulos et al. (2017) also finds significant negative returns for US bidding firms in the three years after a mergers and acquisitions announcement.

While there is evidence that acquiring firms may do poorly after a merger, the targeted company often does much better. On announcement of a merger bid the target firm's share price tends to rise significantly, while the bidding firm's is either more or less unchanged or may decline slightly. The fact that the bidding firm must pay a large sum of money to make an acquisition, while the target firm is to receive money, can explain the different effect on the share price. Another factor is the size differential which usually exists between bidding and target firms, and bidding firms are normally much larger so news has a much smaller effect on their share price than on target firms. But a bigger factor driving the targeted company doing well out of a merger is the competition which often exists between rival firms in bidding, which will push up the price paid to the target firm's shareholders for its acquisition.

There are two different theories of why bidders may bid too high and overpay for their target in mergers and acquisitions; the hubris hypothesis and the self-serving management hypothesis. Roll (1986) explained the hubris hypothesis as the idea that the managers of acquiring firms suffer from excess pride, arrogance and hubris, and this causes them to assume their valuations of target firms are always correct during acquisitions, when in practice they are often mistaken. With rational expectations about those bidding on a target, some can be expected to overbid relative to the actual target's true value, and some are likely to underbid, while the expected true value of the target should be at the mean of the value distribution. But in any acquisition it will be the bidder that makes the highest valuation and is willing to pay the most that will acquire the target firm, not the bidder with the mean valuation, and therefore if there are multiple bidders the winner who acquires the firm will have paid too much. Yet the hubris of acquiring firms' managers will prevent them from seeing this. Roll's hubris hypothesis predicts that shareholders of acquiring firms will see their wealth decline as a result of their managers overpaying, as the shareholders of the target firm sees their wealth increase for the same reason, for an overall result of zero total gains for the combined firm after a merger.

There is some empirical evidence that may support the hubris hypothesis. Rau and Vermaelen (1998) in the US, and Sudarsanam and Mahate (2003) in the UK, find long-term underperformance by acquiring firms after a merger, and blame acquiring firms' overextrapolation of their target's past performance during the bidding process. In other words, acquiring firms are paying too much for the firms they acquire, as they are being overly optimistic about the acquired firms' future profitability and value based on some past performance, which turned out to be temporary. Instead of making a detailed examination of the assets and liabilities of their target companies to determine their true value, managers of bidding firms appear to arrogantly assume that if firms can perform well before they are taken over and without their influence, they will surely perform just as well if not better once they are in charge after an acquisition.

Bhide (1989) provides evidence from the US that firms targeted for hostile takeovers were often poorly performing firms, and this may also support the hubris hypothesis. Overconfident managers of acquiring firms may assume that their management can turn these underperforming firms around, and that their changes will create improvements and facilitate a smooth integration between the merging firms, before a tide of synergies and economies of scale can be enjoyed. But in practice the problems with the target firm may be harder to solve than acquiring managers expected, integration may be difficult, and economies of scale and synergies may prove elusive.

The second hypothesis of why the managers overpay for their targets during acquisitions is the self-serving management hypothesis. This suggests that managers of acquiring firms knowingly and deliberately pay too much during takeovers, as they expect to profit individually from the merger. After an acquisition there is no longer a need for two management teams, and typically the management of the acquired firm often lose their jobs, while the management of the acquiring firm may enjoy a large bonus for completing the merger. If managers know that they can personally secure a sizeable bonus from an acquisition they may be motivated to pursue them, even if it involves bidding too much for target firms which may offer little value. Under the self-serving management hypothesis the bidding firm's shareholders will lose wealth, as the wealth of the target firm's shareholders increases, but after the acquisition value is destroyed as value and wealth is transferred from the combined firm to the management of the acquiring firm.

There is some empirical evidence that may support the self-serving management hypothesis of why acquiring firm managers overpay in acquisitions. Rosen (2004) finds evidence that firms are more likely to undertake frequent acquisitions if their CEOs can expect to gain large compensation increases from acquisitions. A study by Moeller et al. (2005) finds that acquisitions involving firms with extremely high valuations suffer negative synergy gains, but if these firms were to be ignored then acquiring firms' shareholders' wealth would increase with acquisitions. Common sense suggests that firm managers involved in acquisitions with extremely high valuations are more likely to see very high compensation than with lower valuation mergers, as the more money that is spread around the more that will go to acquiring firms' managers on average. Moeller et al.'s study therefore may suggest that lower valuation acquisitions are more likely to be properly thought out, which is why they increase shareholders' wealth in their study, while extremely high valuation acquisitions may not be as thought out and may often just be attempts by acquiring managers to secure a payoff, which is why they generate negative synergy gains in the study.

Looking beyond firm shareholders and management, mergers and acquisitions may create value or they may destroy it. Two groups who are always likely to benefit from mergers and acquisitions are lawyers and investment bankers, as they provide advice and services for those involved in the process and are well compensated in return. Employees at merging firms may not do so well and often suffer job losses after a merger, especially at the acquired firm which may be thinned down and see its assets sold. On the other hand a merger can give a firm greater market power and help it expand and grow in size, creating new jobs and therefore being good for employees. In terms of society as a whole, if a merger increases a firm's market power to the point where it gives it monopoly power, and the firm can do whatever it wants with no competition to keep it in check, then society may suffer a value and welfare loss due to high prices and lower standards. There is therefore a need for regulators to monitor mergers and acquisitions and intervene to prevent them where appropriate. Society can benefit if mergers result in synergy gains however, and more efficient firms with better management can mean lower costs for consumers.

6 Bibliography

Agrawal, A., Jaffe, J. F., and Mandelker, G. (1992) The Post-Merger Performance of Acquiring Firms: A Re-examination of an Anomaly, *The Journal of Finance*, Vol. 47, Issue 4, pp.1605-1621.

Bhide, A. (1989) The Causes and Consequences of Hostile Takeovers, *Journal of Applied Corporate Finance*, Vol. 2, Issue 2, pp.36-59.

Black, F. and Scholes, M. (1973) The Pricing of Options and Corporate Liabilities, *Journal of Political Economy*, Vol. 81, No. 3, pp.637-654.

Brav, A., Graham, J. R., Harvey, C. R., and Michaely, R. (2005) Payout Policy in the 21st Century, *Journal of Financial Economics*, Vol. 77, Issue 3, pp.483-527.

Brounen, D., De Jong, A., and Koedijk, K. (2004) Corporate Finance in Europe: Confronting Theory with Practice, *Financial Management*, Vol. 33, No. 4, pp.71-101.

Giannopoulos, G., Holt, A., Khansalar, E. and Mogoya, P. (2017) The Long-Run Performance of U.S. Bidding Firms in the Post M&A Period: The Impact of Bid Type, Payment Method and Industry Specialisation, *International Journal of Business and Management*, Vol. 12, No. 2, pp.230-245.

Graham, J. R. (2000) How Big Are the Tax Benefits of Debt?, *The Journal of Finance*, Vol. 55, Issue 5, pp.1901-1941.

Graham, J. R., Lang, M. H., and Shackelford, D. A. (2004) Employee Stock Options, Corporate Taxes, and Debt Policy, *The Journal of Finance*, Vol. 59, Issue 4, pp.1585-1618.

Koch, A. S. and Sun, A. X. (2004) Dividend Changes and the Persistence of Past Earnings Changes, *The Journal of Finance*, Vol. 59, No. 5, pp.2093-2116.

Lintner, J. (1956) Distribution of Incomes of Corporations Among Dividends, Retained Earnings, and Taxes, *The American Economic Review*, Vol. 46, No.2, pp.97-113.

Merton, R. (1973) Theory of Rational Option Pricing, *The Bell Journal of Economics and Management Science*, The RAND Corporation, Vol. 4, No. 1, pp.141-183.

Miller, M. (1977) Debt and Taxes, *The Journal of Finance*, Vol. 32, Issue 2, pp.261-275.

Miller, M. H. and Modigliani, F. (1961) Dividend Policy, Growth, and the Valuation of Shares, *The Journal of Business*, Vol. 34, No. 4, pp.411-433.

Modigliani, F. and Miller, M. (1958) The Cost of Capital, Corporation Finance and the Theory of Investment, *American Economic Review*, Vol. 48, No. 3, pp.261-297.

Moeller, S. B., Schlingemann, F. P., and Stulz, R. M. (2005) Wealth Destruction on a Massive Scale? A Study of Acquiring-Firm Returns in the Recent Merger Wave, *The Journal of Finance*, Vol. 60, No. 2, pp.757-782.

Myers, S. C. and Majluf, N. S. (1984) Corporate Financing and Investment Decisions When Firms Have Information That Investors Do Not Have, *Journal of Financial Economics*, Vol. 13, Issue 2, pp.187-221.

Ofek, E. (1993) Capital Structure and Firm Response to Poor Performance: An Empirical Analysis, *Journal of Financial Economics*, Vol. 34, Issue 1, pp.3-30.

Rau, P. R. and Vermaelen, T. (1998) Glamour, Value and the Post-acquisition Performance of Acquiring Firms, *Journal of Financial Economics*, Vol. 49, 2, pp.223-253.

Roll, R. (1986) The Hubris Hypothesis of Corporate Takeovers, *The Journal of Business*, Vol. 59, No. 2, pp.197-216.

Rosen, R. J. (2004) Betcha Can't Acquire Just One: Merger Programs and Compensation, *Federal Reserve Bank of Chicago*, Working Paper No. 2004-22.

Shleifer, A. and Vishny, R. W. (2003) Stock Market Driven Acquisitions, *Journal of Financial Economics*, Vol. 70, pp.295-311.

Stoll, H. (1969) The Relationship Between Put and Call Option Prices, *The Journal of Finance*, Vol. 24, Issue 5, pp.801-824.

Sudarsanam, S. and Mahate, A. A. (2003) Glamour Acquirers, Method of Payment and Post-acquisition Performance: The UK Evidence, *Journal of Business Accounting & Finance*, Vol. 30, Issue 1-2, pp.299-342.

www.ingramcontent.com/pod-product-compliance
Lightning Source LLC
Chambersburg PA
CBHW071410220526
45469CB00004B/1245